Read for a Better World™

I0878819

TRICERATOPS

A First Look

TOM JACKSON

Lerner Publications ◆ Minneapolis

Educator Toolbox

Reading books is a great way for kids to express what they're interested in. Before reading this title, ask the reader these questions:

> What do you think this book is about? Look at the cover for clues.
>
> What do you already know about this dinosaur?
>
> What do you want to learn about this dinosaur?

Let's Read Together

Encourage the reader to use the pictures to understand the text.

Point out when the reader successfully sounds out a word.

Praise the reader for recognizing sight words such as *it* and *was*.

TABLE OF CONTENTS

Triceratops 4

You Connect! 21
STEM Snapshot 22
Photo Glossary 23
Learn More 23
Index 24

Triceratops

Triceratops is a kind of dinosaur. It lived sixty-eight million years ago.

Triceratops
try-SEH-ruh-tahps

It had three sharp horns on its face.

What other animals have horns?

The dinosaur looked like a rhino. But it was as heavy as two rhinos.

The dinosaur had a very big head. It had a parrot-like beak.

It had four short legs.
It had a pointed tail.

The dinosaur was thirty feet (9 m) long.

It ate leaves.

What other animals eat leaves?

The dinosaur used its horns to fight its enemies.

Would you want to find dinosaur bones?

The dinosaur is not alive today. But people find its bones.

The bones teach us
about this dinosaur.

You Connect!

What is something you like about this dinosaur?

What else is as big as this dinosaur?

What other dinosaurs do you know about?

STEM Snapshot

Encourage students to think and ask questions like scientists. Ask the reader:

What is something you learned about this dinosaur?

What is something you noticed in the pictures of the dinosaur?

What is something you still don't know about this dinosaur?

Photo Glossary

beak

bones

horn

rhino

Learn More

Austen, Lily. *Triceratops*. Minneapolis: Jump!, Inc., 2026.

Dittmer, Lori. *Triceratops*. Mankato, MN: Creative Education, 2024.

Vonder Brink, Tracy. *The Triceratops*. New York, NY: Crabtree Publishing, 2024.

Index

beak, 10
head, 10
horn, 6–7
leaves, 14–15
legs, 12
parrot, 10
tail, 12

Photo Acknowledgments

The images in this book are used with the permission of: © Alberto Andrei Rosu/Shutterstock Images, p. 4; © Shan_shan/Shutterstock Images, pp. 7, 23 (horn); © Vladimir Bolokh/Shutterstock Images, pp. 8, 15; © nuwatphoto/Shutterstock Images, pp.9, 23 (rhino); © Eduardo Cabanas/Shutterstock Images, pp. 10, 23 (beak); © Suwat wongkham/Shutterstock Images, p.11; © Orla/Shutterstock Images, p. 12; © Ton PonchaiShutterstock Images, p. 13; © Denis---S/Shutterstock Images, p. 16–17; © LukasKrbec/Shutterstock Images, pp. 18, 23 (bones); © Pao W/Shutterstock Images, p. 20.

Cover Photograph: © Alberto Andrei Rosu//Shutterstock Images

Design Elements: © Mighty Media, Inc.

Lerner Publications Company
An imprint of Lerner Publishing Group, Inc.
241 First Avenue North
Minneapolis, MN 55401 USA

For reading levels and more information, look up this title at www.lernerbooks.com.

Main body text set in Mikado a Medium.
Typeface provided by Hannes von Doehren.

Library of Congress Cataloging-in-Publication Data

Names: Jackson, Tom, 1972–author
Title: Triceratops : a first look / Tom Jackson.
Description: Minneapolis : Lerner Publications, [2026] | Series: Read about dinosaurs: read for a better world | Includes bibliographical references and index. | Audience: Ages 5–8 | Audience: Grades K–1 | Summary: "The triceratops looked similar to today's rhinoceros; horns and all. However, this dinosaur was actually much larger than a rhino. Engaging images and text will teach readers about this interesting herbivore"—Provided by publisher.
Identifiers: LCCN 2025011267 (print) | LCCN 2025011268 (ebook) | ISBN 9798765689783 lib. bdg. | ISBN 9798348029043 pbk | ISBN 9798765697580 epub
Subjects: LCSH: Triceratops—Juvenile literature
Classification: LCC QE862.O65 J295 2026 (print) | LCC QE862.O65 (ebook) | DDC 567.915/8–dc23/eng/20250606

LC record available at https://lccn.loc.gov/2025011267
LC ebook record available at https://lccn.loc.gov/2025011268

Manufactured in the United States of America
1 - CG - 12/15/25